Summary
of

The Last Painting of Sara de Vos
Dominic Smith

Conversation Starters

By BookHabits

Tips for Using BookHabits Conversation Starters:

EVERY GOOD BOOK CONTAINS A WORLD FAR DEEPER THAN the surface of its pages. The characters and their world come alive through the words on the pages, yet the characters and its world still live on. Questions herein are designed to bring us beneath the surface of the page and invite us into the world that lives on. These questions can be used to:

- Foster a deeper understanding of the book
- Promote an atmosphere of discussion for groups
- Assist in the study of the book, either individually or corporately
- Explore unseen realms of the book as never seen before

About Us:

THROUGH YEARS OF EXPERIENCE AND FIELD EXPERTISE, from newspaper featured book clubs to local library chapters, *BookHabits* can bring your book discussion to life. Host your book party as we discuss some of today's most widely read books.

Table of Contents

Introducing *The Last Painting of Sara de Vos*

L inking three lives, on three continents, over a period of three centuries, a rare Dutch painting from the 17th century is the centerpiece of *The Last Painting of Sara de Vos* written by Dominic Smith. The main characters are connected through this painting called "At the Edge of a Wood" —they are all facing choices and circumstances that put them on "the edge" of regret.

The Last Painting of Sara de Vos by Dominic Smith begins over three hundred years ago by introducing the reader to an artist living in Amsterdam with her husband, who is also an artist. During this time, females were usually overlooked as artists and only painted indoor objects like flowers. Transformed by the tragedy of losing her 7-year-old daughter, Sara de Vos decided to defy the expectations of her time and painted a memorable landscape called "At the Edge of a Wood." The painting depicts a young girl staring at skaters on a frozen river. Sara de Vos was eventually recognized as a master painter by the

Guild of St. Luke's in Holland in 1631—she was the first woman to receive this designation.

Fast forward three centuries later to 1957. "At the Edge of a Wood" is the only remaining painting by Sara de Vos, and its owner is Marty de Groot, a wealthy lawyer in New York City; he is a descendant of the original owner of the painting, which has been in his family for a few hundred years. Marty seems to find comfort in the painting. Feeling dissatisfied in his marriage and life in general, he decides he no longer wants to stand on "the edge" and makes decisions he will regret for years to come.

Still in 1957, Ellie Shipley, struggling financially through college, gets entangled in a forgery scheme. She agrees to paint a copy of Sara de Vos' "At the Edge of the Wood," a regrettable decision that will haunt her for many years.

Moving on to the year 2000 in Sydney, Australia, Ellie is enjoying a career as an art expert, specializing in female artists of the Dutch Golden Age. To Ellie, the painting brings inspiration for her career because to her, it represents a woman defying society's expectations. Her career is threatened though when both the forgery she had painted and the original painting are set to arrive for an exhibition at her museum.

The Last Painting of Sara de Vos, a book about art, love, regrets, and life lessons, is a *New York Times* bestseller and Review Editors' Choice, and has been named an Amazon Editors' Top Pick. It was also been named best book by Amazon, *Kirkus Reviews,* the *San Francisco Chronicles,* and *Slate* in 2016. The Independent Booksellers Association in Australia awarded the novel the Fiction Indie Book of the Year. It was also named the Literary Fiction Book of the Year at the Australian Book Industry Award.

Much research went into the writing of the book because the author wanted to be certain it was historically accurate. He learned what it was like to be a woman during the Golden Age. He also conducted interviews with experts to learn about art restoration and conservation, as well as art forgery.

In an interview with the *Chicago Tribune,* Dominic Smith said that he became interested in painters of the Golden Age while he was living in Amsterdam. He realized that there were "missing layers of the Dutch Golden Age," which prompted him to begin writing the book. He said that art in the Golden Age was similar to literature, in that it was "interconnected" and "it all had value." Smith also said he was interested in exploring why the art world feels so strongly about forgery.

Readers will not only be entertained by the story but will also learn so much about Dutch art, especially female painters of the 17th century—Sara de Vos is a fictional character that blends the styles of real-life Dutch painters. The author gives readers a lesson in art history, as well as construction. Dominic's inspiration for Sara de Vos was a Dutch artist named Judith Leyster. Leyster became one of the rare instances that a woman entered the Haarlem Guild of St. Luke. Because of the restrictions of female artists of the time, her work was originally attributed to Frans Hals.

The Last Painting of Sara de Vos is currently available in Paperback, Hardback, eBook, and Audiobook.

The book has received rave editorial and reader reviews since its release. According to *Kirkus Reviews,* the book is a "beautiful, patient, and timeless." *The Australian* calls the book "deeply researched, beautifully written, and intellectually absorbing."

Discussion Questions

"Get Ready to Enter a New World"

Tip: Begin with questions dealing with broader issues to ensure ample time for quality discussions. Read through all discussion questions before engaging.

~~~

question 1

The painting seemed to be one of the main characters of the book. How did your perception of the painting change throughout the book?

~~~

~~~

question 2

Art seems to be a popular topic in contemporary fiction these days, with books like *Girl with a Pearl Earring* and *The Goldfinch*. Compare and contrast *The Last Painting of Sara de Vos* with one of these art-focused novels.

~~~

~~~

question 3

The author links three lives, on three continents, over a period of three centuries. How well do you think he was able to pull these different aspects together? Did the book flow well from time to time, place to place, and person to person?

~~~

question 4

Sara de Vos was transformed by the tragedy of losing her 7-year-old daughter. In what ways did this influence her art?

~~~

question 5

The title of the painting is "At the Edge of a Wood." How the title relate to each of the three main characters—Sara, Marty, and Ellie?

~~~

~~~

question 6

In the 1950s, Ellie created a forgery of the painting. Do you think it takes talent to do this well? Do you consider forgery an art form? Why or why not?

~~~

~~~

question 7

The painting depicts a young girl staring at skaters on a frozen river. What meaning/imagery does this painting portray to you?

~~~

~~~

question 8

The book seems to have a feminist tone in regards to the characters Sara de Vos and Ellie Shipley. Did you notice this tone while you were reading? Compare and contrast the two main female characters.

~~~

question 9

Regarding the relationship between Marty and Ellie, how do you think
forgery and illusion shaped their relationship?

~~~

question 10

The author gave readers a lesson in art history and construction. What did you learn about art by reading this book?

~~~

~~~

question 11

Each of the characters in the book was married. Discuss the success (or lack of) of those relationships and how they related to the painting.

~~~

~~~

question 12

Both Ellie and Sara are facing sexism, but in different ways. Discuss the
differences about the sexism they faced in each of their time periods. Do you
think women face the same kind of sexism today?

~~~

~~~

question 13

Regarding the sexism addressed in the previous question, what do you think empowered the two women to pursue their careers in a world dominated by men?

~~~

~~~

question 14

A lot of research went into writing the book because the author wanted to be certain it was historically accurate. How well do you think Smith did in portraying the time and events accurately?

~~~

~~~

question 15

During the time de Vos was painting, females were usually overlooked as artists and only painted indoor objects like flowers. Why do you think this was the case?

~~~

~~~

question 16

The book has received rave reviews and won a number of awards. Do you think this is all hype or is the book worthy of all its praise?

~~~

~~~

question 17

Several reviewers appreciated the art lesson they received. Do you agree?
What did you learn about art techniques or processes that you didn't know
before reading the book?

~~~

~~~

question 18

A few reviewers criticized the characters, saying they were "pretentious."
What did you think of the characters? Were they appropriate for the story?

~~~

~~~

question 19

Smith decided to begin the project of writing this book after he realized that there were "missing layers of the Dutch Golden Age." Do you think he did a good job of filling in the missing pieces about the Dutch Golden Age? Why or why not?

~~~

~~~

question 20

Some reviewers have criticized the accuracy of the information regarding art conservation techniques. How much does it matter whether or not the artist portrays everything accurately, considering it is a fiction novel?

~~~

Introducing the Author

Dominic Smith is an award-winning author from Australia. He was born and raised in Sydney but currently lives in Austin, Texas. He graduated with a masters of fine arts from the Michener Center for Writers at the University of Texas – Austin. He has taught at the University of Texas, Southern Methodist University, and Rice University. He is currently on the graduate fiction faculty at the Warren Wilson College Masters of Fine Arts Program for Writers.

Dominic Smith writes both historical and contemporary fiction, bringing them together in one book. He is known for being able to coax the past to life. *The Last Painting of Sara de Vos* is Smith's latest novel about Dutch art in the Golden Age. Smith has also written three other novels, including his first novel *The Mercury Visions of Louis Daguerre* (2006), a historical novel about photography; *The Beautiful Miscellaneous* (2007), a novel about a father's expectations of his son; and *Bright and Distant Shores* (2011), a historical novel about skyscrapers set in 1890s Chicago and the South Pacific. Smith has also written for a variety of publications, including *The New York Times, the Chicago Tribune,* and *The Atlantic Monthly.*

Dominic Smith has won many awards for his writing, including the Sherwood Anderson Fiction Prize and the Gulf Coast Fiction Prize. He also received a grant from the Australian Council for the Arts. His work has been shortlisted for two of Australia's leading literary awards, the Vance Palmer Prize and The Age Book of the Year.

When asked about what he finds to be the most difficult part of the writing process, Smith said that revision is the hardest part. He finds it difficult to "kill off things that are holding back the book," of which he said it takes willfulness and discipline to do. Smith tells aspiring writers to read "widely and deeply" if they want to be a good writer. Also, he tells aspiring writers to experiment with form and voice. Regarding writer's block, Smith says you shouldn't wait for inspiration to strike; he believes writing is "muscular" and "requires a regimen."

Dominic Smith said he enjoys reading older books, such as *In the Skin of a Lion* by Michael Ondaatje and *The Left-Handed Woman* by Peter Handke.

Dominic Smith is in the process of researching for his next novel, which will be another historical fiction, this time about American filmmaking. Smith says that he likes writing historical novels because he enjoys the research, which affords him the opportunity to engage experts.

Fireside Questions

"What would you do?"

Tip: These questions can be a fun exercise as it spurs creativity among the readers by allowing alternate scene endings and "if this was you" questions.

~~~

question 21

Dominic Smith often combines contemporary and historical fiction together.
Does this "mashup" appeal to you? Why or why not?

~~~

~~~

question 22

Dominic Smith says he enjoys researching historical novels because he gets to engage experts. What do you think your favorite part of the writing process and why?

~~~

~~~

question 23

Dominic Smith is originally from Australia. In what ways can you see his Australian upbringing in his writing, if at all?

~~~

~~~

question 24

Dominic Smith is in the process of writing his next novel, which will be about American filmmaking. Are you looking forward to this novel? Why or why not?

~~~

~~~

question 25

Dominic Smith says he finds it difficult to "kill off things that are holding back the book" when referring to revision. Why do you think this is so difficult for some writers?

~~~

~~~

question 26

Ellie's decision to forge Sara de Vos' painting seemed a desperate one because she didn't feel she had a choice. If you were in the same position as Ellie, would you have made the same choice? Why or why not?

~~~

~~~

question 27

The book linked three lives, in three different places, in three different time periods. How do you think the story would be different if the events took place all in modern day?

~~~

~~~

question 28

Sara de Vos painted "At the Edge of a Wood" after the death of her daughter.
If you lost a child at such a young age, what would your painting look like?

~~~

question 29

Ellie was the art forger in the 1950s. How do you think the story would be different if she were a male?

~~~

question 30

If you could take the place of one of the three main characters in the book, who would it be and why?

~~~

Quiz Questions

"Ready to Announce the Winners?"

Tip: Create a leaderboard and track scores to see who gets the most correct answers. Winners required. Prizes optional.

~~~

quiz question 1

Sara de Vos was a Dutch painter from the _____

century.

~~~

~~~

quiz question 2

True or False: The painting was called At the Corner of Elm.

~~~

quiz question 3

Sara de Vos living in _____ with her husband.

~~~

quiz question 4

True or False: Sara's daughter passed away at birth.

~~~

~~~

quiz question 5

Marty de Groot was a wealthy lawyer who lived in
_____.

~~~

~~~

quiz question 6

True or False: Ellie Shipley got entangled in a forgery scheme in the 1950s.

~~~

quiz question 7

In the year 2000, Ellie had become an art expert, specializing in female artists
of the _____.

.

~~~

quiz question 8

True or False: Dominic Smith was born and raised in Sydney, Australia.

~~~

~~~

quiz question 9

Dominic Smith graduated from the University of Texas with a masters of
_____.

~~~

~~~

quiz question 10

True or False: Dominic Smith writes historical fiction and non-fiction books.

~~~

~~~

quiz question 11

Dominic Smith's next book is set to be about _____.

~~~

~~~

quiz question 12

Dominic Smith's first book is called _____.

~~~

Quiz Answers

1. 17th
2. False; it was called At the Edge of a Wood
3. Amsterdam
4. False; she was 7 years old
5. New York City
6. True
7. Dutch Golden Age
8. True
9. fine arts
10. False; he writes historical and contemporary fiction.
11. American filmmaking
12. The Mercury Visions of Louis Daguerre

Ways to Continue Your Reading

E VERY month, our team runs through a wide selection of books to pick the best titles for readers and reading groups, and promotes these titles to our thousands of readers – sometimes with free downloads, sale dates, and additional brochures.

Want to register yourself or a book group? It's free and takes 1-click.

Register here.

On the Next Page...

Please write us your reviews! Any length would be fine but we'd appreciate hearing you more! We'd be SO grateful.

Till next time,

BookHabits

"Loving Books is Actually a Habit"

Made in the USA
Las Vegas, NV
14 March 2021

19541602R00033